The Root of 'oot'

'oot'

b

Word Play

By: AJ Crigler

The Root of 'oot'

By: A J Crigler

The Root of 'oot'

Artwork and story by: A J Crigler
StoryTime Publications
P.O. Box 1644
Miamisburg, OH 45343-1644

ISBN-13: 978-0615972916
ISBN-10: 0615972918

This book was printed in the United States of America.

To order additional copies of this book, contact: AJ Crigler at

email: ajcstorytimepublications@aol.com

The Root of 'Oot'
By: A J Crigler

This is a little story

about a root called 'oot.'

and you can hear O--O--T,

when a train whistle goes toot.

The train goes up a steep hill

and leaves a trail of black soot.

The engine is stoked with coal

with a shovel from the coal shoot.

What words have crossed

our paths so far ending in O--O--T?

Root, toot, soot, and shoot,

and there are others to see.

roōt

toōt

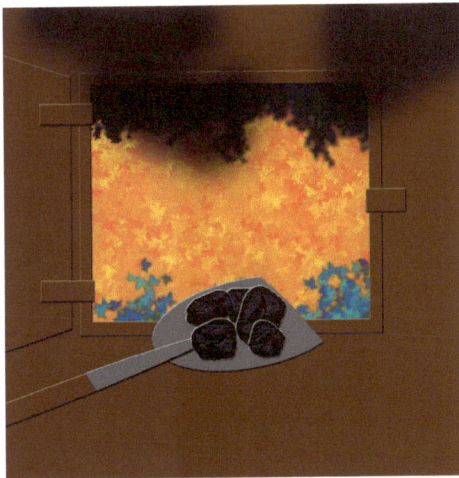

soŏt

shoōt

Some 'oots' are long and some are short

like soot as well as foot.

The oo's can make two different sounds

and to argue the point is moot.

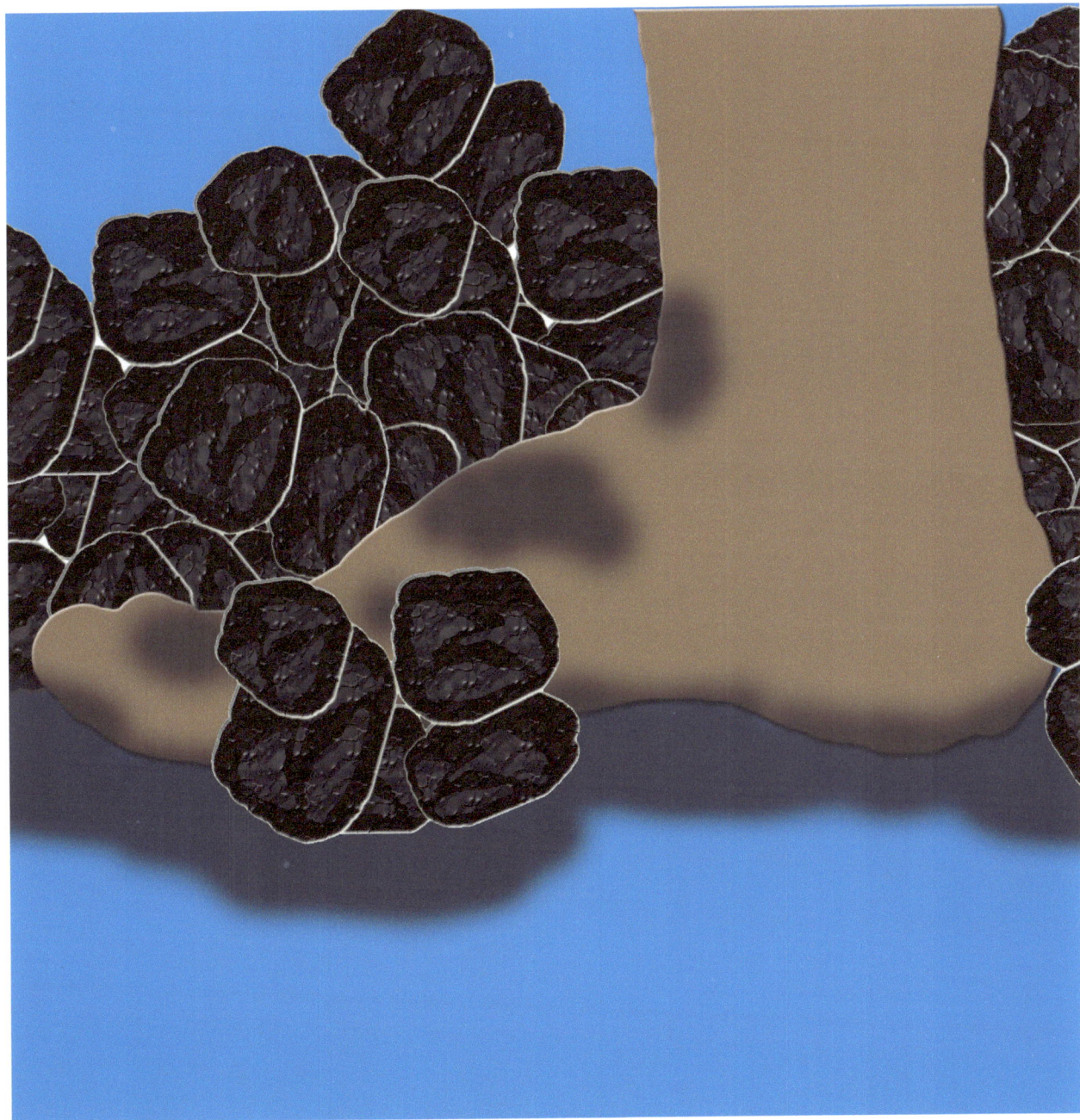

There's an owl in a tree

and he says hoot, hoot

every time the train whistle

goes toot, toot, toot.

hoot

hoot

Seven words in all,

if there is no dispute.

Root, toot, soot, shoot,

foot, moot, and also hoot.

root

toot

hoot

shoot

moot

foot

soot

The next word on our route

is just a word to suit

the cargo that we are hauling,

which is a lot of loot.

Our next stop is a bank

to take the loot back

from where it was first stolen

by a bandit on the track.

Boot City Bank

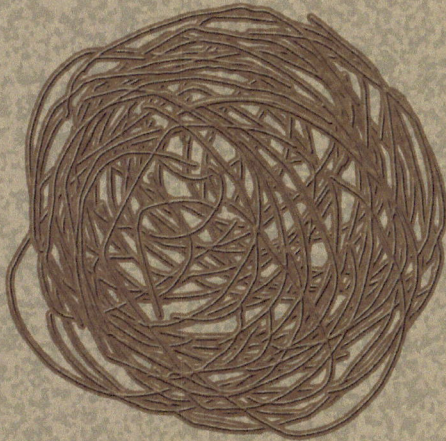

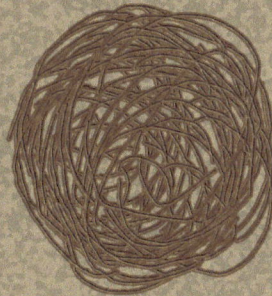

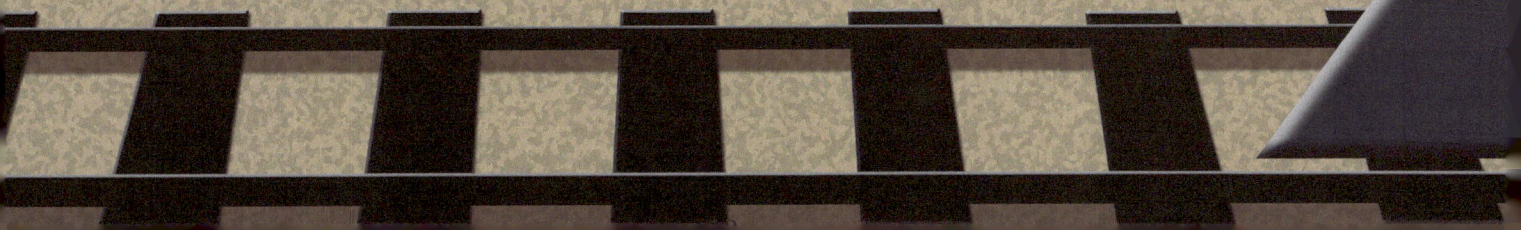

The bandit was also caught

and delivered with the loot,

by a sheriff named Oot,

who caught him and did not shoot.

The hero of the story

is the brave sheriff 'Oot.'

So, if trouble comes your way

do not give 'Oot' the boot.

'oot'

Let's round up all the words

and give a big salute.

I have found nine in all

to show and then let's scoot.

root

toot

hoot

shoot

boot

moot

foot

soot

scoot

The End

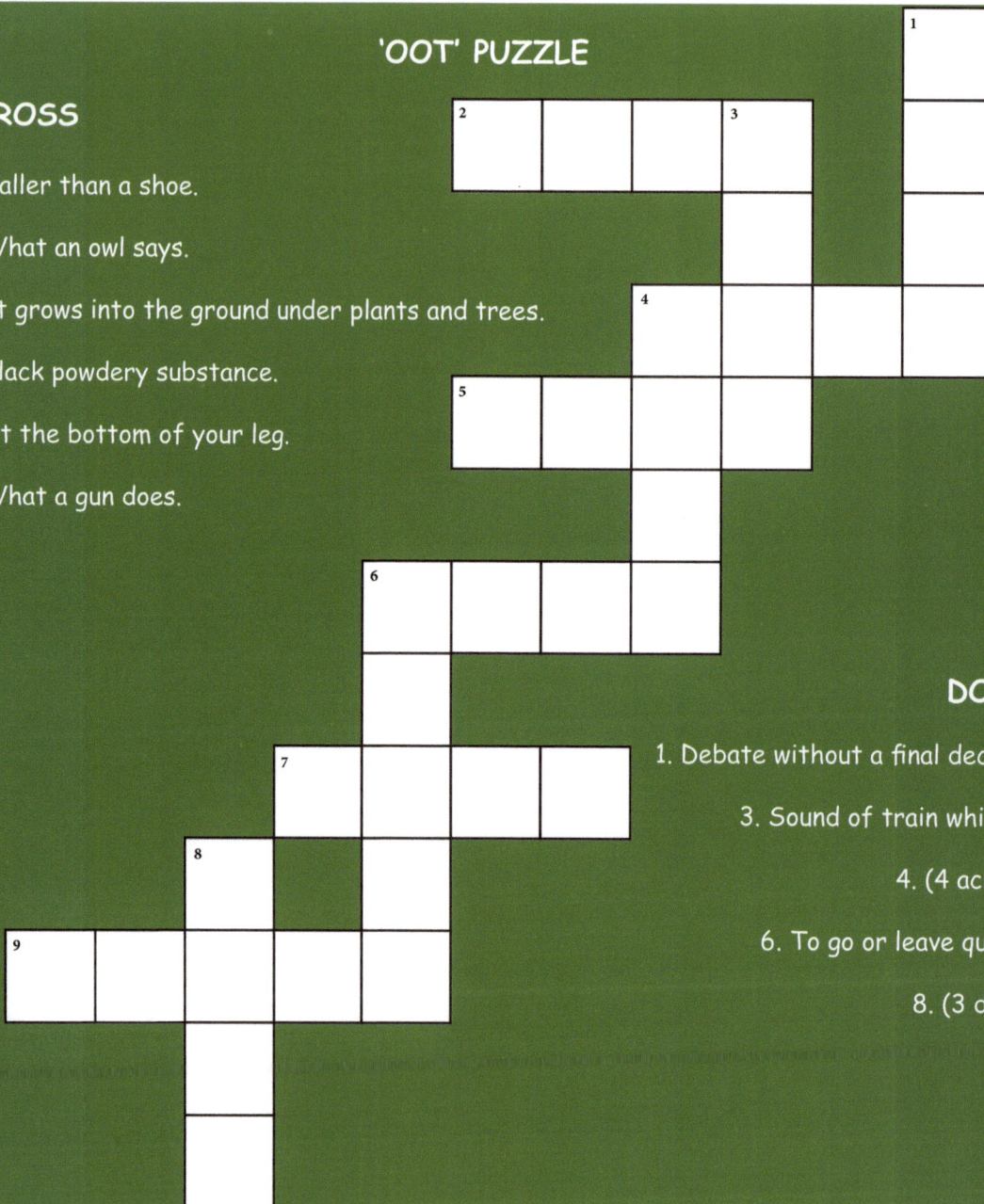

'OOT' PUZZLE

ACROSS

2. Taller than a shoe.

4. What an owl says.

5. It grows into the ground under plants and trees.

6. Black powdery substance.

7. At the bottom of your leg.

9. What a gun does.

DOWN

1. Debate without a final decision.

3. Sound of train whistles.

4. (4 across).

6. To go or leave quickly.

8. (3 down).

PUZZLE ANSWERS

ACROSS

2. Taller than a shoe.

4. What an owl says.

5. It grows into the ground under plants and trees.

6. Black powdery substance.

7. At the bottom of your leg.

9. What a gun does.

DOWN

1. Debate without a final decision.

3. Sound of train whistles.

4. (4 across).

6. To go or leave quickly.

8. (3 down).

						¹M
²B	O	O	³T			O
			O			O
			⁴H	O	O	T
⁵R	O	O	T			
			O			
⁶S	O	O	T			
C						
⁷F	O	O	T			
⁸T		O				
⁹S	H	O	O	T		
O						
T						

The Root of 'oot'

The Root of 'oot' (TROO) is a book of word play that is the second edition of the word play series. This edition is focused on words that end in o-o-t. **TROO** is a story for children 6-12 and also some adults.

   Writing and illustrating **TROO** was fun. It was exciting to develope pictures to go with the rhymes. It is a fictional fantasy and I hope everyone will enjoy **TROO** as much as I did creating it.

   Reading is essential to life.

Story Time
Publications

www.ingramcontent.com/pod-product-compliance
Lightning Source LLC
Chambersburg PA
CBHW040232070426
42447CB00030B/159